BEAUTIFUL

JOURNEY THROUGH
the
Human
BODY

Brain

and the nervous system

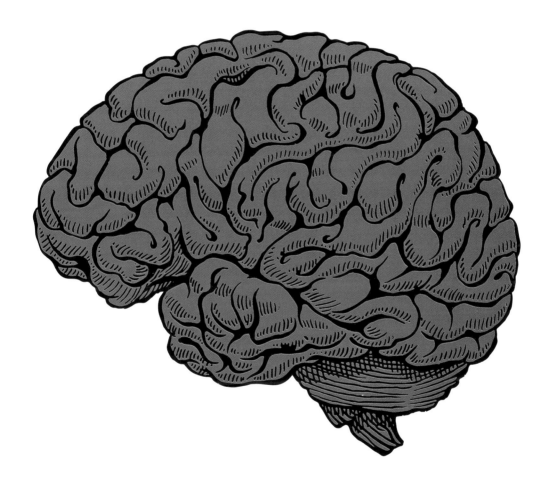

By
Charlie Ogden
Designed by Danielle Jones

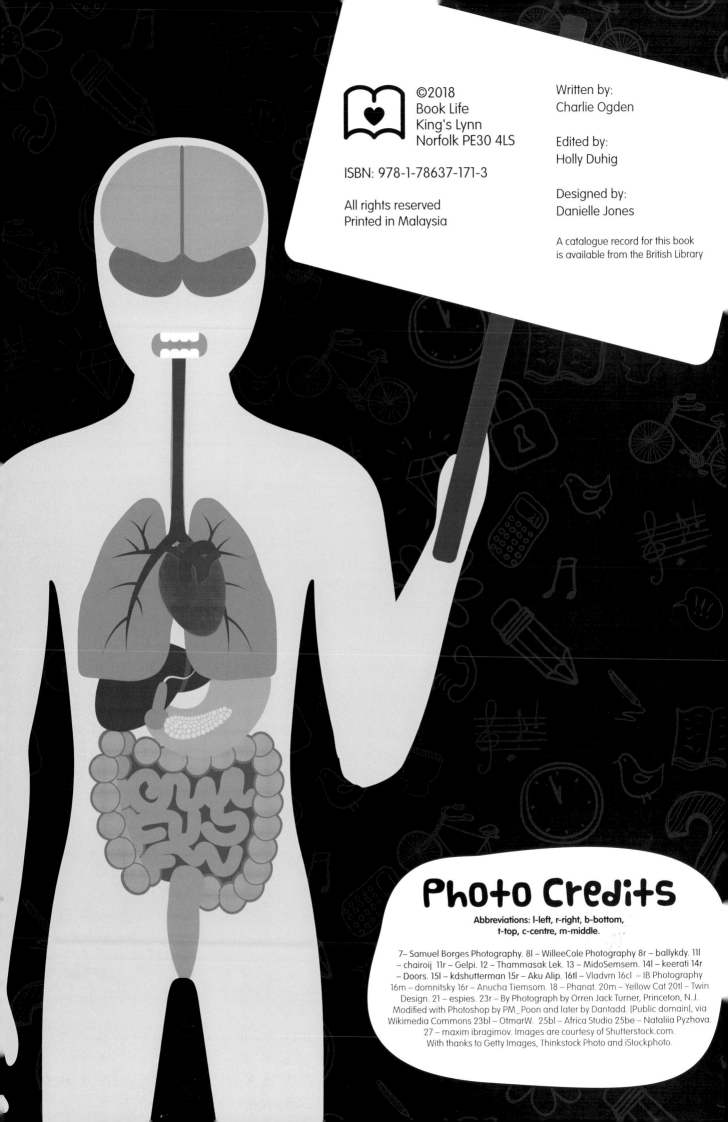

©2018
Book Life
King's Lynn
Norfolk PE30 4LS

ISBN: 978-1-78637-171-3

Written by:
Charlie Ogden

Edited by:
Holly Duhig

Designed by:
Danielle Jones

A catalogue record for this book
is available from the British Library

Photo Credits

**Abbreviations: l-left, r-right, b-bottom,
t-top, c-centre, m-middle.**

7– Samuel Borges Photography. 8l – WilleeCole Photography 8r – ballykdy. 11l – chairoij 11r – Gelpi. 12 – Thammasak Lek. 13 – MidoSemsem. 14l – keerati 14r – Doors. 15l – kdshutterman 15r – Aku Alip. 16tl – Vladvm 16cl – IB Photography 16m – domnitsky 16r – Anucha Tiemsom. 18 – Phanat. 20m – Yellow Cat 20tl – Twin Design. 21 – espies. 23r – By Photograph by Orren Jack Turner, Princeton, N.J. Modified with Photoshop by PM_Poon and later by Dantadd. [Public domain], via Wikimedia Commons 23bl – OtmarW. 25bl – Africa Studio 25be – Nataliia Pyzhova. 27 – maxim ibragimov. Images are courtesy of Shutterstock.com. With thanks to Getty Images, Thinkstock Photo and iStockphoto.

BEAUTIFUL Brain

and the nervous system

CONTENTS

Hi, I'm Dr. Brian Cell. Follow me to start your journey through the nervous system!

Words that look like **this** are explained in the glossary on page 31.

The HUMAN BODY

The human body is very complicated. The body is full of **organs**, bones, **muscles** and blood and all of these parts are wrapped up in a thin layer of skin. Because of this, finding your way around the human body can be very difficult and dangerous if you don't have a guide.

But lucky for you, I am here – so let our journey begin!

There are over **75 ORGANS** in the **HUMAN BODY!**

Systems of the Body

The first thing that you need to know about the human body is that it uses **systems**. The systems of the body are made up of groups of organs that work together.

Each system of the body has its own important job to do, such as stopping the body from getting sick or helping to keep the body strong.

There are lots of different systems in the body, but some are more important than others. Four of the most important systems in the body are:

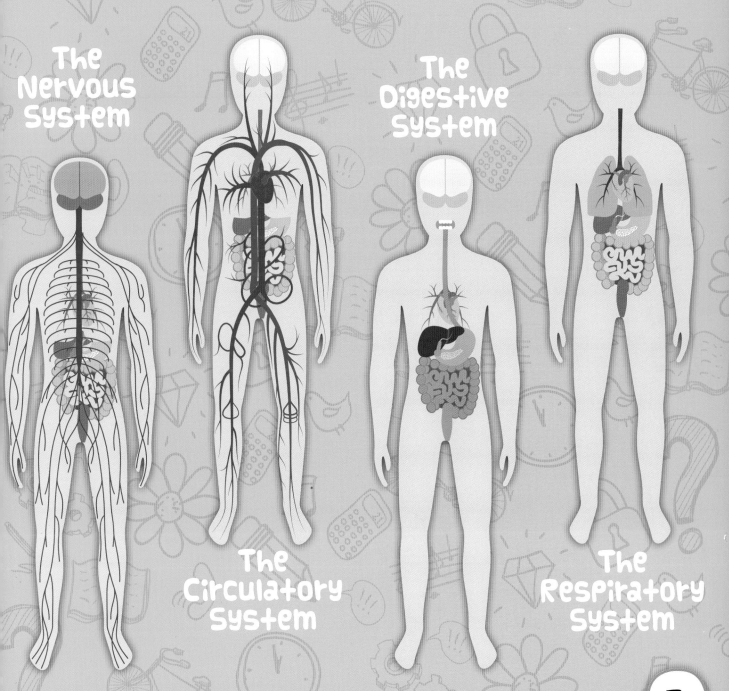

The Nervous System

The Digestive System

The Circulatory System

The Respiratory System

The NERVOUS SYSTEM

The main organ in the nervous system is the brain. The brain is a very complex organ and it controls the entire body, from moving the **limbs** to pumping blood through the heart.

However, it does far more than just control the body. Intelligence, **creativity**, speech and emotion are just a few of the more unusual and complicated things that the brain is responsible for.

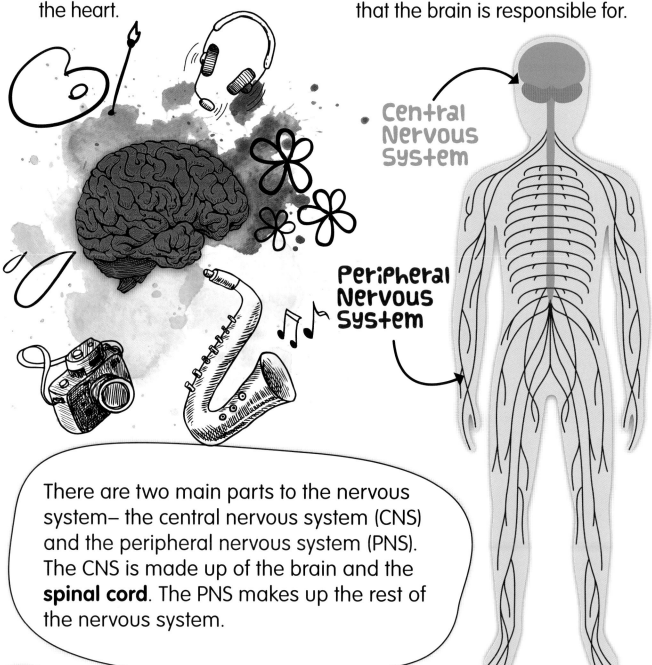

Central Nervous System

Peripheral Nervous System

There are two main parts to the nervous system– the central nervous system (CNS) and the peripheral nervous system (PNS). The CNS is made up of the brain and the **spinal cord**. The PNS makes up the rest of the nervous system.

Your PNS collects all sorts of information from your body. Information about what you're seeing, tasting, smelling, hearing and feeling is all collected by the PNS.

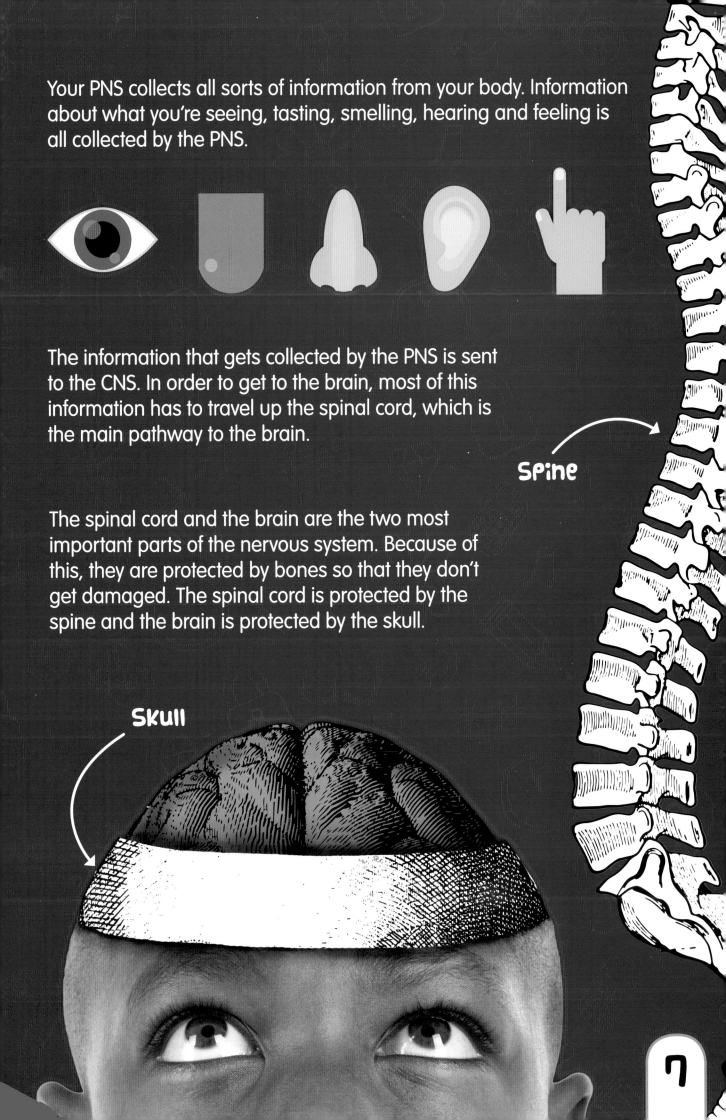

The information that gets collected by the PNS is sent to the CNS. In order to get to the brain, most of this information has to travel up the spinal cord, which is the main pathway to the brain.

Spine

The spinal cord and the brain are the two most important parts of the nervous system. Because of this, they are protected by bones so that they don't get damaged. The spinal cord is protected by the spine and the brain is protected by the skull.

Skull

MIND MAPS

There are three main parts to the brain: the cerebrum, the cerebellum and the brainstem. Each of these parts has its own set of complicated and important jobs to do.

Cerebrum

Cerebellum

Brainstem

The brainstem sits right at the base of the brain and it is the smallest of the brain's three main parts. The brainstem controls things that are very important for keeping the body working. This includes things like your **heart rate**, breathing, **digestion** and body temperature.

Lots of animals have brainstems that are very similar to human brainstems. This is because the brainstem controls things that nearly all animals, including humans, need to do.

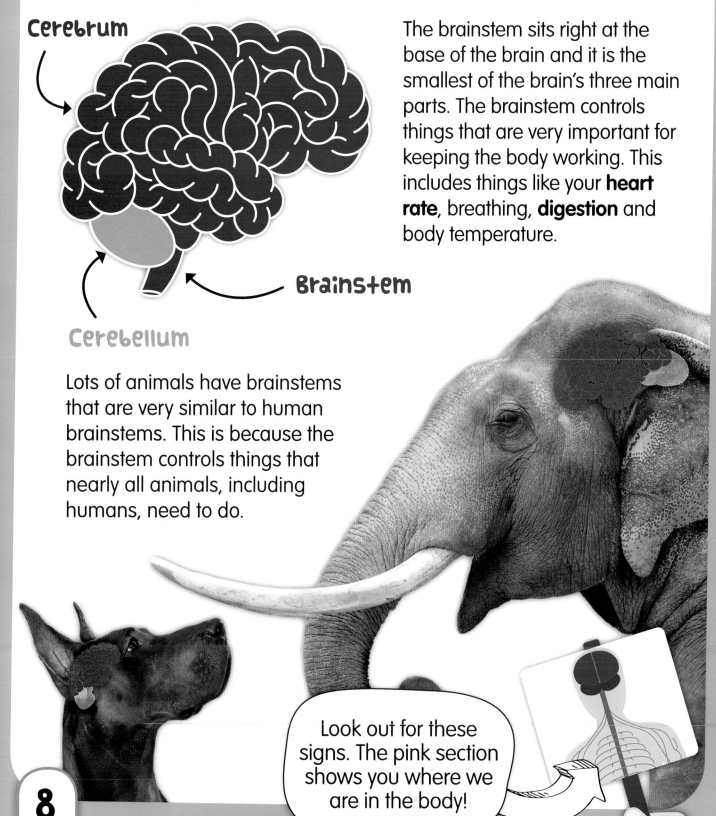

Look out for these signs. The pink section shows you where we are in the body!

Come on, cerebellum!

The main job of the cerebellum is to control how the body moves. Whether you clap your hands or stamp your feet, your cerebellum is doing the work. This part of the brain also controls your balance.

Your cerebellum also controls the movement of your mouth and **voice box**, meaning that it controls your speech. It also helps you to understand written words. So, without your cerebellum, you couldn't be reading this book!

The final part of the brain is the cerebrum. This is the largest part of the brain and it has a groove down the centre that splits it into two halves. These halves are called hemispheres.

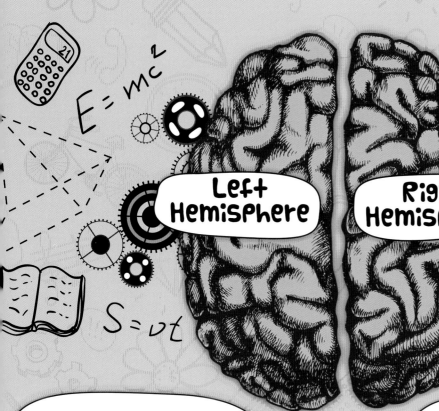

Left Hemisphere

Right Hemisphere

The left hemisphere of the cerebrum deals better with numbers. Strangely, it has more control over the right side of the body.

The right hemisphere of the cerebrum deals better with creative tasks, such as making art. Strangely, it has more control over the left side of the body.

9

LOBE-TROTTING

The cerebrum can also be split into an inner section and an outer section. The inner section is responsible for a lot of important things that help to keep us alive and healthy. The outer section, called the cerebral cortex, is where most of the fun stuff happens!

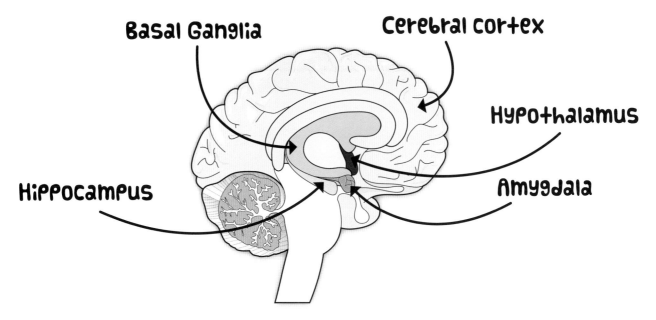

Basal Ganglia

Cerebral Cortex

Hypothalamus

Hippocampus

Amygdala

Each of the cerebral cortex's hemispheres can be split up into four sections called lobes. The four lobes are; the frontal lobe, the parietal lobe, the occipital lobe and the temporal lobe.

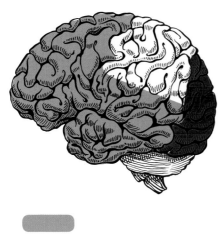
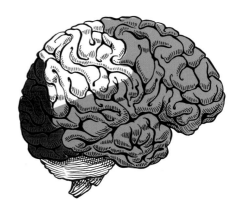

Frontal Lobe

Occipital Lobe

Temporal Lobe

Although each hemisphere of the brain is split into four lobes, these lobes do not work alone. Nearly everything that the brain does involves complex connections between different lobes in both hemispheres of the brain.

FRONTAL LOBE

The frontal lobe sits at the front of the brain. It is responsible for a lot of your creativity and for your **personality**. Intelligence comes from this part of the brain, as do emotions, problem-solving skills and a bunch of other things.

PARIETAL LOBE

One of parietal lobe's main jobs is to control the sense of touch. The sense of touch is very important as it helps us to feel temperature and pain, both of which help the body to know when it is damaged or in danger. This lobe also helps the brain to understand words and language.

OCCIPITAL LOBE

The occipital lobe has one of the hardest jobs in the entire body – controlling our sight.

Think about how quickly you throw up your hands to protect your face when someone throws something at you. In the time that it takes for your hands to fly up, your occipital lobe has received information from the eyes and has worked out what you're seeing. It has also worked out that, unfortunately, you're about to get hit in the face. It then sends all this information to the rest of the brain so that your hands will **automatically** fly up and protect you.

Around **30%** of the CEREBRAL CORTEX deals just with **SIGHT.**

It only takes 0.05 seconds for the brain to take in information from the eyes and build up a picture of what you're seeing.

TEMPORAL LOBE

The temporal lobe has many jobs, but one is more important than the rest.

The word 'temporal' means 'to do with time'. This part of the brain is called the temporal lobe because it is responsible for memories and the way that we think about time.

The temporal lobe is involved with creating long-term memories. These are the memories you have of things that happened a long time ago.

The memories that we have of things that happened long ago often come with a picture – you often remember what it was like to see something happen. This is because the temporal lobe uses information from your eyes to help create long-term memories.

You've got SOME NERVES

The peripheral nervous system has one main job – sending information to and from the brain.

The brain needs information about the body to make the best decisions about what to do next. After the brain has responded to the information it gets, messages about what to do next need to be sent all over the body. All this is done by the PNS.

For the PNS to do its job properly, it has to spread to every inch of the body. The parts of the PNS that can sense different things, such as heat or pain, are called sense receptors. There are many different types of sense receptor in the body and each of them can sense different things. There are sense receptors in your eyes, on the bottom of your feet and even in your bones.

Sense receptors are not spread evenly across the body. Some parts of the body have lots of sense receptors, whereas others only have a few.

Lips

Many Receptors

Leg

Some Receptors

Elbow

Few Receptors

The most common type of sense receptor in the body is called a free nerve ending. Free nerve endings are mostly found in the skin and they sense temperature, **pressure**, stretching and pain. All this together makes up your sense of touch.

There are lots of sense receptors in the lips and the mouth and this makes these parts of the body very **sensitive**. This helps us to know when our mouth is being damaged, for example, when you eat something that's very hot. It is important that the mouth doesn't get damaged as this could make it difficult to eat.

FIND YOUR SENSITIVE SIDE

There's a simple test that you can do at home to see just how sensitive different areas of your skin are! All you need for this test is a paperclip, a ruler, a pen and a piece of paper.

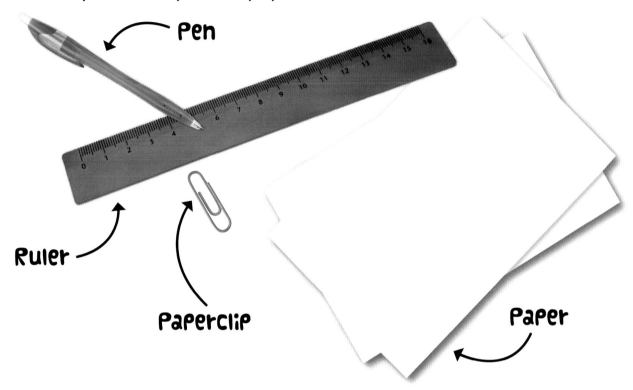

Pen

Ruler

Paperclip

Paper

First things first, you are going to need to think about all of the different areas of skin that you want to test. Write down all the different body parts you want to test on your piece of paper.

Then, you are going to need to bend your paperclip into a U-shape. For this experiment, we need both ends of the wire next to each other and pointing the same way.

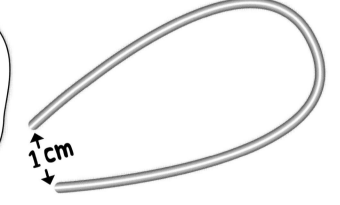

1 cm

Bend the paperclip wire so that the two ends are about one centimetre apart. Use your ruler to help you to do this. Now, lightly press the two ends of the paperclip against different parts of your body.

RESULTS

You should find that the sensitive parts of your body can feel both ends of the paperclip, but that less sensitive areas of skin cannot tell the two ends apart. In these cases, it feels like just one point is being pressed against the skin.

If you want to be a real scientist, make the gap between the ends of the wire a bit smaller. Then see where on your skin you can still feel the two separate points. Keep making it smaller and smaller to find your most sensitive areas of skin!

BE CAREFUL!

Ask an adult to help you with this test! The two ends of the paperclip might be a little sharp, so do not put them anywhere near your eyes, mouth or ears.

COMMUNICATION BREAKDOWN

The body is made up of tiny units called **cells**. Different cells make up different parts of the body. For example, the blood contains blood cells and the skin contains skin cells. The cells that make up the nervous system are called neurons.

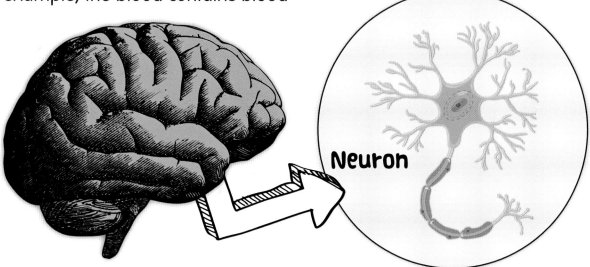

Neuron

Neurons carry messages between different parts of the brain and between the brain and the body. When you feel a burning pain in your hand, neurons in your nervous system send this message to the brain. When your brain wants you to move your hand away from the thing that's burning you, neurons send this message to the muscles in your arm and hand.

There are lots of different types of neuron. However, there are two particular types of neuron that are more important than the rest.

Sensory neurons send information from the body to the brain. These neurons gather information about your body and the world around you and send this information to the brain. They are called sensory neurons because they collect information from your senses.

Motor neurons are like the brain's very own messaging service. They send messages from the brain to the body. 'Motor' means 'to do with movement or motion'. Messages sent from the brain using motor neurons usually result in the body performing an action, such as catching a ball or taking a deep breath.

There are over 100,000,000,000 **NEURONS** in the human body.

Some messages get sent through the nervous system very quickly. However, others can take much longer.

Some messages need to be sent through the nervous system extremely quickly. This is usually because they protect the body from something that's going to happen very soon! These messages are sent through the nervous system at over 400 kilometres per hour!

Other messages take a lot longer to travel through the nervous system. One of the main reasons that this happens is because the messages aren't as important for keeping the body alive.

One message that takes a long time to travel through the nervous system and be acted on by the brain is the message from the stomach saying that it is full.

Before you start eating, your brain receives lots of messages from your stomach saying that it is empty and that you need to start eating.

Dear Brain

EAT!

LOVE STOMACH
xxx

EAT!

EAT!

EAT!

EAT!

EAT!

STOP EATING!

After you have eaten enough fo[od], a new message needs to be se[nt] to tell the brain to stop eating. T[he] message that you are full gets [sent] to the brain when sense recept[ors] in the stomach sense that the stomach has stretched and is n[ow] full of food.

However, this message doesn't reach the brain for a long time. This is because other parts of the body, such as the intestines, are still sending messages to the brain telling it to eat. With all these different messages being sent

to the brain, it can take up to 2[0] minutes for the brain to realise [that] the stomach is full and that you should stop eating.

It is best to **EAT SLOWLY**. This way, you won't eat too much food before the **MESSAGE** to stop eating reaches your **BRAIN**!

FEEL the LEARN

When neurons send messages to muscles in the body, all they need to do is send the message to the correct muscle. After that, the job is done! However, this is not enough when you're trying to learn something.

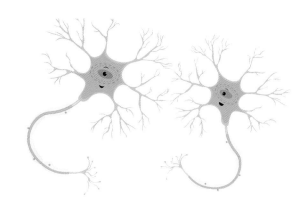

To learn something, a message must be sent from one neuron in the brain to another neuron in the brain over and over again. By sending the same message between the same neurons over and over – for example, by reading the same part of a textbook over and over – the connection between these two neurons gets stronger and stronger.

Come on, brain. Make those connections stronger!

When the connection between two neurons in the brain is very strong, it becomes very easy for messages to be sent between the neurons. This is what it means to have learnt something!

This picture shows what the brain looks like under a **microscope**. You can see lots of connections between different neurons.

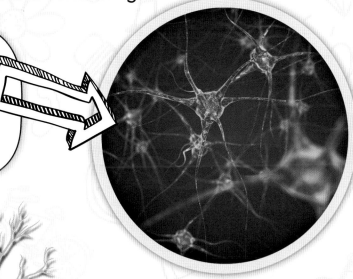

Is it the 14th of March?

Yes! You remembered!

Let's say you learnt that Albert Einstein's birthday was the 14th of March. If someone asked you when his birthday was, a message would be fired between two particular neurons in the brain and you would remember what you've learnt. The stronger the connection between those two neurons, the more quickly and easily the message would be sent.

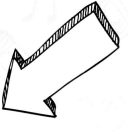

Albert Einstein

We learn lots of important things, such as walking and talking, when we are very young. This is possible because babies' brains are very good at making new connections. As you get older, it becomes harder to make new connections. So it's best to learn as much as you can while you're young!

COME to your SENSES

Your five senses are possibly the most important things that your nervous system is responsible for.

We have already looked at the sense of touch: here we will explore taste, smell, sight and hearing.

TASTE

Different tastes are detected by your taste buds. There are over 10,000 taste buds on your tongue.

Taste

Taste Pore

Before you can taste food, it needs to mix with the **saliva** in your mouth. This helps **particles** of food to get washed down into the tiny gaps in your tongue. Your taste buds are found in these tiny gaps.

Taste Bud

Tongue

Neurons

Your taste buds can only detect five different tastes. All the different flavours that you can think of – from strawberry milkshake to fried bacon – are made up of a mixture of the five tastes that your taste buds can detect. The five tastes are:

Sour

Salt

Bitter

Sweet

Umami

SMELL

The body needs the sense of smell so that it can work out if something is food or not. Things that smell bad are usually bad for you and shouldn't be put in your mouth.

When you take a big sniff, air rushes into your nose and fills up your nasal cavity. However, it's not just air that goes into your nasal cavity – tiny particles of different things also enter your nose.

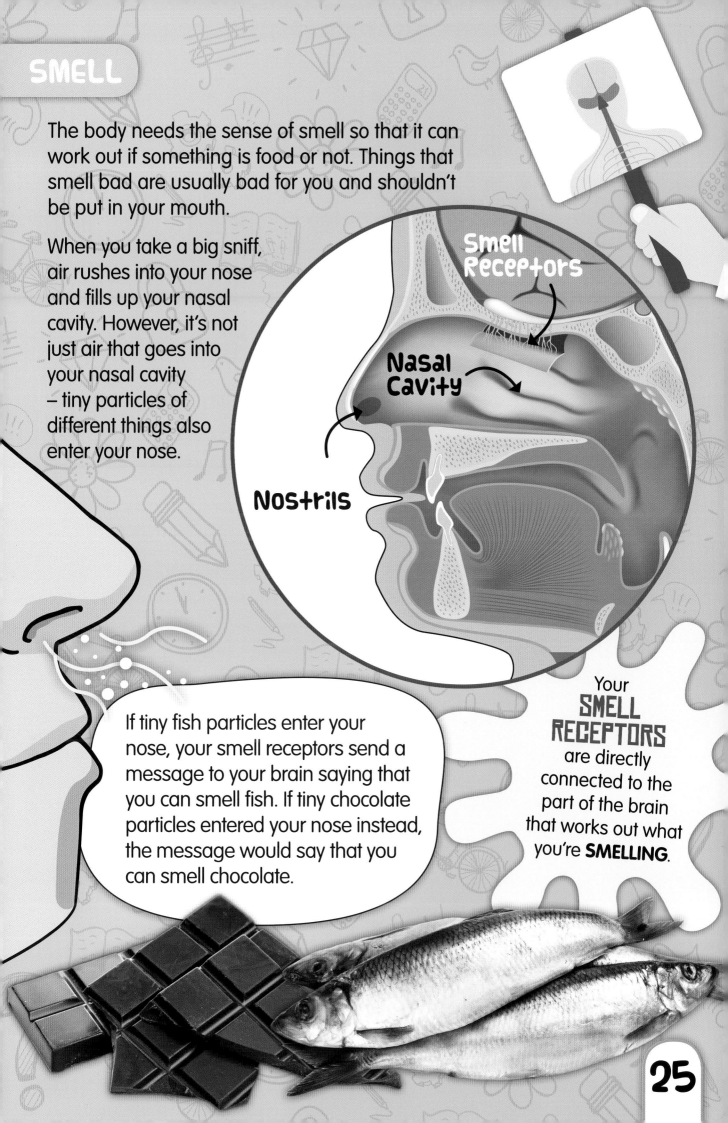

Smell Receptors

Nasal Cavity

Nostrils

If tiny fish particles enter your nose, your smell receptors send a message to your brain saying that you can smell fish. If tiny chocolate particles entered your nose instead, the message would say that you can smell chocolate.

Your **SMELL RECEPTORS** are directly connected to the part of the brain that works out what you're **SMELLING**.

SIGHT

The main sense receptors in the eyes, called cones, sense different colours of light. The cones send information about the light that enters the eyes to the brain.

This information gets sent to the brain along the optic nerve. The brain uses this information to build up a picture of the world around you.

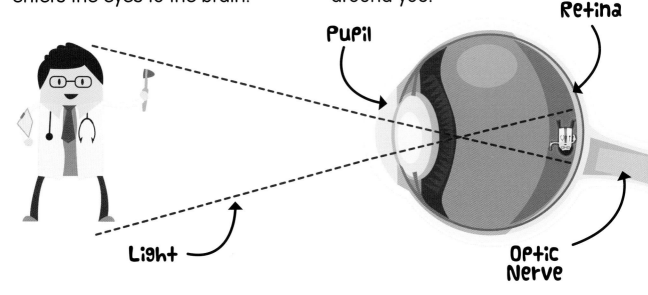

Retina

Pupil

Light

Optic Nerve

In order for you to see an object, light must bounce off it and then enter your eye through your pupil. The light will be different colours depending on the colour of the object that it bounced off.

An upside-down image of the object you are seeing is then projected on the retina, which is where the eye's light-sensing cone receptors are.

There are three light-sensing cones in the eye, one that is best at sensing red light, one that is best at sensing green light and one that is best at sensing blue light.

Sounds are tiny **vibrations** that travel through the air. The body senses these vibrations using the eardrums, which are little discs of tightly stretched skin in your ears. When vibrating air enters your ears, it makes your eardrums vibrate as well.

The outside part of the ear, known as the auricle, helps to push vibrations in the air into the **ear canal** and towards the eardrum. The eardrum vibrates with the air and passes on these vibrations to parts of the ear that are deep inside the skull.

The vibrations are passed down through the ear until they reach tiny hairs deep inside the skull. Sense receptors connected to these hairs sense the vibrations and send information about them to the brain. The brain uses this information to work out the sounds that are being heard.

BRAIN Training

1. The brain compares the images it gets from the eyes against it's memory banks. This helps it to work out what's being seen.

I've seen you before!

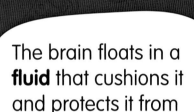

2. The brain floats in a **fluid** that cushions it and protects it from getting damaged.

3. A baby's brain doubles in size in the first 90 days that he or she is alive.

Day 1

Day 90

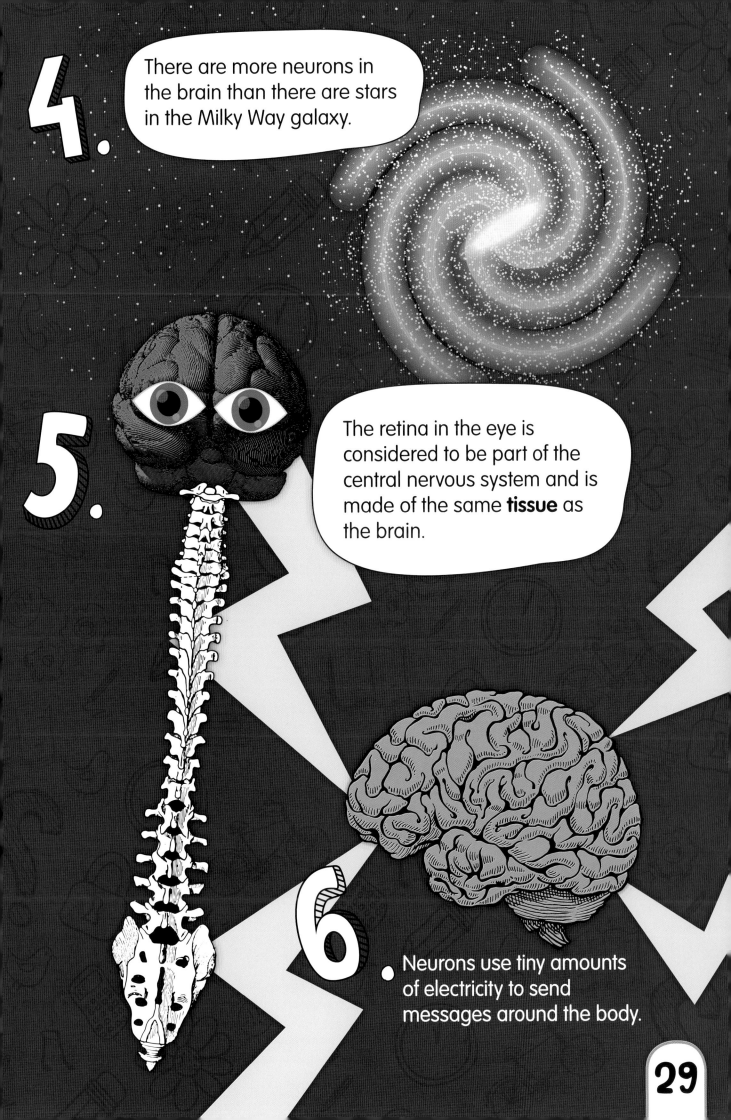

TEST your NERVES

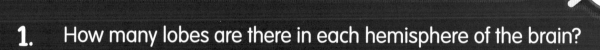

Use what you've just learnt to try to answer these questions. The answers are upside down at the bottom of the page.

1. How many lobes are there in each hemisphere of the brain?

2. What does the temporal lobe help to create?

3. What protects the brain from getting damaged?

4. What are the sense receptors in the eyes called?

5. What is the auricle?

6. What are the most common sense receptors in the body?

7. What are the two main parts of the central nervous system?

8. How many different tastes can your taste buds sense?

9. Which neurons send messages from the brain to the body?

10. Which neurons send information from the body to the brain?

Answers: 1. Four 2. Long-term memories 3. The skull 4. Cones 5. The outside part of the ear 6. Free-nerve endings 7. The brain and the spine 8. Five 9. Motor neurons 10. Sensory neurons

30

GLOSSARY

automatically   without conscious thought or control

cells   the basic units that make up all living things

creativity   using imagination and new ideas to create something

digestion   the process of digesting food

ear canal   the tube that runs from the outer part of the ear to the inner part of the ear

fluid   a substance that flows, especially a liquid

heart rate   the speed at which your heart beats

limbs   arms and legs

microscope   an instrument used by scientists to see very small things

muscles   bundles of tissue that can contract or squeeze together

organs   parts of the body that have their own specific jobs or functions

particles   very small pieces of matter

personality   the combination of qualities that make up a person's character

pressure   the physical force of being pressed

saliva   a watery liquid made by glands in the mouth

sensitive   quick to detect and respond to damage or injury

spinal cord   the long, thin bundle of nerves that are encased in the spine and send messages to the brain

systems   sets of things that work together to do specific jobs

tissue   any type of material that a living thing is made out of, including humans

vibrations   small, shaking movements

voice box   the organ in the throat that helps people to speak

INDEX

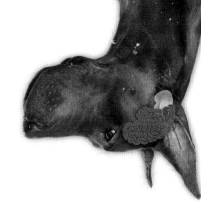